In the name of Allah—
The Most Gracious, The Most Merciful

be *soft,*
be strong

Inspirational Reminders
for Muslim Women

kashmir maryam

www.strangeincorporated.org
www.kashmirmaryam.com

www.strangeincorporated.org
www.kashmirmaryam.com

Published by Strange Inc, a nonprofit publishing house based
in New York. Our mission is to elevate the authentic voice of
Muslim women.

This book may be purchased for educational, business, or sales
promotional use. For more information, please e-mail the
marketing department at hello@strangeincorporated.org

Interior illustrations by Aleena Masroor
Book cover design by Kashmir Maryam
Interior formatting by Leo Baquero

ISBN 979-8-9888848-1-1 (paperback)
ISBN 979-8-9888848-2-8 (hardcover)

*for she who yearns to soften her heart
and strengthen her emaan*

contents

be wise

Something beautiful happens when we loosen the reigns that tie us to this transient worldly life. Remember, if we care too much about other people's perception of us—we have already *lost* our power.

Take, for instance, the act of leaving home while wearing the *hijab*[1]. The veil gives us dignity—it distinguishes and separates us from the crowd. It may ignite inspiration in some, *but it might not sit so well with others*. The truth is that no matter what we do in life, there will always be both supporters *and* critics. This is an inescapable aspect of life. However, once we achieve inner peace with our Creator, the ceaseless quest for validation is quenched.

---

1. In the Islamic context, the *"hijab"* refers to the modest dress code and behavior observed by Muslim women as a reflection of their faith. It involves covering the body and hair in the presence of non-*mahram* (non-related) men to promote modesty, privacy, and adherence to Islamic principles. The hijab is not only a form of clothing but also a religious symbol that signifies a woman's commitment to her faith and her desire to maintain dignity and modesty in her interactions with others.

Incredible transformations occur when we shift our focus from what other people think to what Allah[2] (swt[3]) thinks of us. So free yourself from the burden of societal expectations and return to that which gives you *meaning and life*.

---

2. "Allah" is the Arabic term for God. In Islam, Allah (swt) is believed to be the one and only deity, the creator of the universe, and the ultimate source of guidance for humanity.

3. The letters "swt" are an abbreviation for the Arabic phrase "subhanahu wa ta'ala," which is commonly used by Muslims when referring to Allah (swt). Translated to English, "subhanahu wa ta'ala" means "Glory be to Him, the Exalted." Muslims often include this phrase as a sign of respect and reverence when mentioning the name of Allah (swt), recognizing His transcendence and greatness.

*To envision tomorrow's success,
first look to today's friends.*

Do not be surprised when you begin to witness a shift in your life the moment you take a step toward Allah (swt). Life often cradles us in a cocoon of comfort, shielding us from the subtle changes that slowly harden our hearts over time. We might be left wondering: *why has my heart lost the softness it once felt?* But the moment you add value to your life through the remembrance of Allah (swt) is the moment that the transformation begins to take place.

Remind yourself to embrace these waves of change, because your Creator is positioning you somewhere better—*just trust Him.*

Social media may lead you to believe that you are falling behind everyone else. *You are not*. You are exactly where you are supposed to be. Allah (swt) knows in His infinite wisdom what is best for His servants—His timing is impeccable.

When you are more spiritually conscious, you will find that the signs are *everywhere*. These bespoke signs can take many forms. Through the words or actions of others. Through the answering of prayers. Through the unexpected closing of some doors—and the miraculous opening of others. Throughout all of this, you will find that Allah (swt) is guiding and teaching you something.

Embrace this journey with an open heart and a receptive mind—and stay vigilant of the signs that He is sending your way.

kashmir maryam

You may have a loyal "fan base" or supportive friends around you—but the moment you move into your value system and are unafraid of expressing that (for the sake of Allah (swt)), you may notice these same trusted individuals turning against you. *Suddenly you feel strange.* Suddenly you are perceived as self-righteous. Suddenly you feel out of place.

Let the life of the Prophet Muhammad[4] (pbuh) remind you that once *you* change, the people around you will also change—for better, or for worse.

---

4. Prophet Muhammad (pbuh), also known as Muhammad ibn Abdallah, was the last prophet and messenger in Islam. Born in Makkah (in present-day Saudi Arabia) around 570 CE, he received revelations from Allah (swt) through the angel *Jibreel* (Gabriel), which were later compiled into the Islamic holy book—the Quran. Muslims say "peace be upon him" (pbuh) after mentioning Prophet Muhammad's name as a sign of respect and admiration. This phrase is a way for Muslims to convey their reverence for the Prophet (pbuh) and to invoke blessings upon him.

You are not responsible for anyone else. Allah (swt)
will ask each of us what we put forward in terms of our
deeds. Once you have accepted this truth, you will live
a more peaceful existence.

Beware of how you treat the people around you—they may be the only ones who stick around in your time of need.

The best time of your life is *now*. The best moments are passing you by every day. The "dream" is not what you are working toward. It is the here—*the now*. Make it count.

if we become
the ocean
the seas
have no option
but to merge
with us

i have had to learn
with time
that an unclear answer is
also an answer—
in *not* knowing
there is knowing

every earthly force
whispers the same wisdom:
stay humble
and grounded
like Adam and Hawa[5]—
even gravity
is teaching you where
Allah (swt) placed you

---

5. In Islam, the story of Adam and Hawa ("Eve" in English) parallels the biblical narrative, albeit with some distinctions in the details. They were given free will, and Allah (swt) provided them with clear instructions. However, they were tempted by *Shaytaan* (Satan) and ate from the forbidden tree. As a result, they were expelled from paradise and sent to earth.

If you are constantly trying to fit into other people's framework of "success"—*you will always fail*. Why? Because their framework is always changing, and usually depends on their subjective understanding. Instead, seek Allah's (swt) guidance and align it with your personal values to create a vision for yourself. Then, follow that vision with unwavering determination, tapping into the wisdom He has blessed you with.

When you need a thing more than it needs you,
be wary of how much you attach yourself to it.

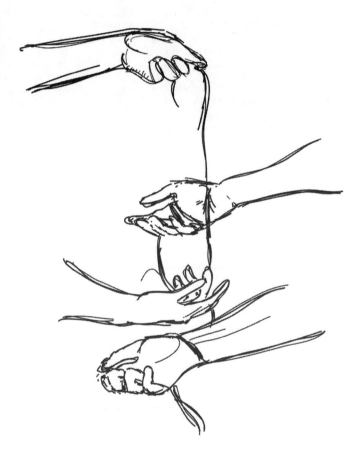

Ten timeless life lessons:

1. I do not fear the consequences of speaking my truth, as long as I am not brash or ignorant in my mannerism.
2. I know that opportunities lie in Allah's (swt) hands. In surrendering to Him, I release all fear and anxiety.
3. I do not ask of creation with rigid expectation, only with hope.
4. If someone closes their door upon me after I knock three times, I move to another door, for *they* were not my people.
5. When I am invited, I accept, except to that which displeases my Lord.
6. My destiny can be influenced by *dua*[6].
7. No one can supplicate against me if I am on the side of justice. My destiny is already woven—I am only living it out.
8. I know that purity can wash over me only when I have made my heart lenient on the people, but stern on myself.
9. I know I cannot move the needle of time, just what I do with the grains of sand slipping through its fingers.
10. I am here, ready to extend peace—but absent if you misuse it.

6. "*Dua*" is an Arabic term that translates to "supplication" or "invocation" in English. In the context of Islam, *dua* refers to the act of calling upon Allah (swt) in prayer or making a request, expressing one's needs, desires, and seeking guidance. It is a fundamental aspect of Islamic worship and personal connection with God. *Dua* can be made in any language and at any time.

Oh Allah, do not leave me to my vices. You are not in need of me—*I am in need of You*. Oh Allah, I stand on the crutches of faith. I know you will not disappoint me, but I do not know how much I will disappoint myself. I am tethered to the crucifix, with my ego nailed through each palm and the crown of *shaytaan*[7] sits heavy on the head of the one who divides the family.

---

7. "*Shaytaan*" refers to the devil or Satan in Islamic theology. It is often used to describe the primary rebellious entity, Iblis, who refused to bow to Adam (as) and, as a result, was cast out of paradise. The term is also more broadly used to refer to evil forces or demonic beings that seek to lead humans astray from the path of righteousness in Islam.

When the world becomes a selfish place, you will begin to appreciate those who are sincerely there for you—without any ulterior motive. Allah (swt) placed those people in your life for a reason. *Cherish them.*

As I journey through the memories of my childhood self and contemplate the dreams I once held close, I come to a profound realization: the life I now lead surpasses anything I could have ever envisioned. This revelation isn't rooted in the mere completion of a checklist (I have certainly not fulfilled every item on my life's bucket list!). Rather, it arises from the intricate tapestry of experiences—the twists and turns that have guided me to my present life. In this journey, I recognize Allah's (swt) Divine plan at work. And without a doubt, the challenges, and trials that He bestowed upon me have been the *key* to shaping the person I have become today.

When you understand that your loved ones are on loan to you—and not permanent beings who will be around forever, *everything* changes.

If you try to resist *qadr*[8], you will find yourself on a tough road that, by its nature, will never be blessed. However, when you embrace Divine decree (the "good" and the "bad" of it), the challenging path can turn into a smoother journey.

---

8. "*Qadr*" is an Arabic term in Islam that translates to "destiny," "fate," or "divine preordainment." In Islamic belief, *qadr* refers to the concept of Allah's (swt) predestination or Divine will. It encompasses the belief that everything that happens is according to the will and plan of Allah (swt); it is one of the fundamental beliefs in Islamic theology.

Books can be written on the steps to achieve success—
but the truth is, success ultimately comes from Allah
(swt). So do what He loves, and refrain from that
which He dislikes. *You will undoubtedly find success.*

When a person asserts
their boundaries—*respect them.*

Every single experience in your life is *gifted* to you by Allah (swt). He is building you up. He is shaping you into who you need to become. And remember, that every hardship or pain you have felt *serves a purpose*. Undoubtedly, The One who brought you to it, will guide you through it too.

some days require fire

some days require water

some days require silence

some days require waves

They tell you to envision what you can attain, and then "manifest" it. But imagine if you focused on all the things that you *already* possess—wouldn't that be the most powerful thing of all?

For years, you may have asked Allah (swt) for things that would have been destructive to you. But in His wisdom, He granted you what was better—even if your heart could not fully comprehend the wisdom behind it at the time.

Remind your heart that even when withholding something from you, Allah (swt) is The Most Kind. Remind your heart to be at peace with that which He gives, *and* that which He chooses to protect you from.

Do not underestimate the profound impact of toxic energy on your overall well-being. Toxic individuals are as common as the air we breathe. And it is essential to remember that you have control over *who* and *what* you allow into your life. Your heart, being the most important part of your spirituality, *must* be safeguarded. Allowing people to corrupt it or allowing your own negative thoughts and actions to do so essentially allows the poison to permeate your entire being.

In Islam, we find Allah's (swt) guidance echoing this sentiment. Allah (swt) says, "Oh you who have believed, protect yourselves and your families from a Fire whose fuel is people and stones" (The Quran, 66:6). This verse underscores the importance of guarding not only our own hearts but also those of our loved ones from negative influences.

Your spiritual insight shall guide you through the labyrinth of *shaytaan's* deception. With steadfastness, you *will* rise above the shadows of doubt that he tries to cast on your path. In those moments especially, hold onto the rope of Allah (swt). By default, your dependence on Him *alone* will leave no option but to illuminate your path toward Him.

It is easy to place the blame of negative occurrences on "evil eye" and on "haters." What is harder to accept is Divine decree (*qadr*)—the good of it and the bad of it. Yes, evil eye is real. Yes, it is true that haters in your inner circle are an impediment to your success. However, to acknowledge the factors *within* your control is much more empowering and much more drastic in overcoming defeat. Otherwise, you will live an existence blaming everything *except* yourself for the trajectory of your life. Indeed, it is a mighty task to face the flaws within yourself, and it requires a great deal of bravery to challenge yourself to become better.

Our past experiences serve as invaluable lessons when we deeply reflect upon them. These trials become intricately woven into the tapestry of our life's journey, guiding and shaping us into the individuals we are destined to be. They serve as tests of our faith, forging our character, and reminding us of the profound importance of placing our trust in Allah (swt).

Success has no gatekeepers. When it aligns with Allah's (swt) will, you *will* reach the station He has destined for you. *No one can take away what is already written for you.* Furthermore, if you chase after a dream contrary to His plan, no matter how hard you try, you will never attain it.

Do not presume that merely because someone sees goodness in you they will automatically treat you with kindness. The nature of humans is complex. This also serves as a perfect reminder that our intentions and actions are ultimately judged *only* by Allah (swt). So we should strive to treat others well, irrespective of their perceptions of us.

It never ceases to amaze me that according to Allah's (swt) Divine wisdom, He not only builds you up in front of those who sought to tear you down, but He *also* unveils to you the repercussions that those with ill-intentions face as a result of that.

Choosing righteous company is akin to investing in yourself and your hereafter. Just as a rose may share its fragrance with you, good company imparts its virtues. The Prophet Muhammad (pbuh) emphasized the significance of surrounding ourselves with those who strengthen our connection with Allah (swt) and inspire us to lead a life in accordance with His guidance. Such virtuous companionship will not only nurture your soul, but also help steer you along the path of righteousness, serving as a constant reminder of the ultimate goal: pleasing Allah (swt).

If you believe that people will always remain consistent and dependable, you are bound to be disappointed. I solemnly swear by the One who fashioned this soul that the sole source of unwavering consistency in our lives is Allah (swt) alone.

It is rare to find someone who "has it all." Someone may own a house, but not a home. Some faces are beautiful, but they mask immeasurable pain. Some parents have five or more children—all of whom are disrespectful and defiant. Some children have both parents alive, yet do not return any of their calls. Some people have three sources of revenue but lack *barakah*[9] in their wealth. Others have luminous eyes but lack the capacity for foresight. Some have the voice of an angel but carry around a ghastly mannerism.

There is wisdom and balance in the way that Allah (swt) has dispersed His blessings among His creation. We must honor the strengths that we *do* possess and be humble enough to accept that *no one has it all.*

---

9. In Islam, "*barakah*" denotes Divine blessings and abundance from Allah (swt). *Barakah* brings prosperity and positive outcomes in various facets of life, such as health, wealth, and relationships.

The presence of the Quran in one's life is irreplaceable. It is transformative. Its effects are undeniable. And once it permeates the human heart, *it changes everything*. It carves a luminous trajectory in the life of the believer, infusing each step with purpose and meaning. It gifts its reader with peace and tranquility. What more can the searching heart ask for?

Do not live with the hope that tomorrow is promised to you. "*What if?*" will bring you sorrow. But "what now?" will bring you relief.

The past has forsaken you, but the future chases you. Of all, your loyal companion is the present, so do not abandon it.

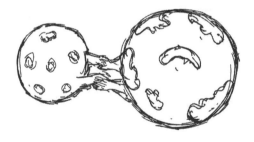

Fame is temporary and deeply unfulfilling. *It is disloyal to the heart that craves it.* It chases you when it is least desired. And it departs when the heart finally embraces and enjoys it. Instead, seek to be known by those in the heavens—not those upon the earth.

Engaging in virtuous deeds should not be contingent upon external validation from others. Doing good deeds should stem from a commitment to righteousness driven inherently by the want to please Allah (swt)— not to receive praise from people.

though the storm brews
and swirls around you—
be still

Feeling emotional triggers indicates that there are lingering wounds within you that await healing. *This is natural.* Remember, you are only human. In those moments, remind your heart to turn to Allah—*Al-Shafi* (The Healer)—to seek solace and remedy for these inner wounds. In prayer and reflection, you will find the strength to entrust your journey toward healing to the ultimate source of compassion—Allah (swt).

It is a most profound realization that as a writer, our words do not originate from us—they flow *through* us. This is also a poignant reminder that all goodness originates from Allah (swt), whereas any weaknesses and imperfections are the result of our own actions and choices.

you will find that
the most beautiful
form of anything is
born at a time of
survival

The heart intuitively knows *who* will best console it. Sometimes an unexplainable bond forms with a person. This connection is all a part of Allah's (swt) plan—He guides us to the souls that we inherently recognize.

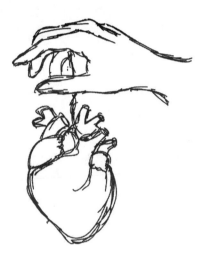

Confidence is sometimes mistaken for arrogance by those who have not fully embraced it. And self-worth is oftentimes misinterpreted as conceit. Striking a balance and nurturing these qualities with humility is important. But *true* confidence and self-worth stem from a deep connection with Allah (swt) and a sense of purpose in serving His greater plan. In trusting Him, you will find everything you need.

I am a true believer in that a person who does good in this life will see some of the good signs and rewards for that effort in this very life—as well as in the hereafter. Allah (swt) says:

"Is the reward for good [anything] but good?"
(The Quran, 55:60)

This verse emphasizes the principle that those who do good deeds will be rewarded with good, reflecting the concept of Divine justice and recompense in Islam. *Alhamdulillah.*

Conversely, a person who does evil will feel the punishment of their wrongdoing both in this life as well as the hereafter. Allah (swt) tells us:

"Evil (sins and disobedience of Allah, etc.) has appeared on land and sea because of what the hands of men have earned (by oppression and evil deeds, etc.), that Allah may make them taste a part of that which they have done, in order that they may return (by repenting to Allah, and begging His Pardon)."
(The Quran, 30:41)

When you stand by someone in their moment of difficulty, they will remember you for a lifetime.

I would often skim over the details regarding Prophet Nuh[10] (as) constructing the ark on *dry* land. But when I deeply reflected over this, I was stunned by how profound this apparently "small" detail is. His unwavering faith meant that despite the dry land, he knew the rains would come (as Allah (swt) promised), and he took action based on that faith. This teaches us that even when we lack complete knowledge or cannot foresee the path ahead, we should still have faith and *do* something. This requires that we have deep trust in Allah's (swt) plan, knowing that He will guide us to where we need to be.

10. "Nuh" refers to the prophet Noah in Islamic tradition. The "(as)" after the Prophet Nuh's name is an abbreviation derived from the Arabic phrase "*alay-hi-salaam*," which translates to "peace be upon him" in English. This term is commonly used as a sign of respect when referring to the prophets in the Islamic tradition.

Do not raise children to placate your feelings. Instead, instill respect and the ability to discern right from wrong based on Allah's (swt) guidance, rather than human fallibility. Raise children who speak the truth out of their *connection with Allah* (swt)—not out of fear of you.

.

When you feel a sudden shift toward compassion for someone—whether you know them or not, *go with it*. Make a prayer for that person. And even if you do not fully understand the reason why they crossed your mind, just remember that *Muqallib Al-Quloob*[11] (The Turner of Hearts) turned your heart for a reason.

---

11. "*Muqallib al-Quloob*" is an Arabic phrase that translates to "The Turner of Hearts" in English. This is one of the attributes of Allah (swt) in Islamic tradition. The phrase reflects the belief that Allah (swt) has the power to change and guide the hearts of individuals.

i beheld my sins
as vast as the sea
—they appear to me—
but I remember
Allah's favors.
then like the stars
cradled in darkness,
my soul found
its flight

be prudent

A believer who is firmly grounded in their faith is never truly alone. They recognize that in their solitude from people, they find companionship with The Most High. Their trust in Him is unshakable—and their reliance upon Him is unwavering.

kashmir maryam

When you view your relationships as if they are an *amaana* (a trust)—and not just as a mere avenue for personal gain, *everything changes.*

how can i remind my soul,
that i am worthy enough to lead it?
as a shepherd guides their flock—
i am the guardian of my body and soul.

i must remember that the light is one
but the darknesses are many.
that judgment awaits—
like the space between two fingers.

how do i impress upon my hands—
each with its unique print
that they will one day testify
and their identity is within my grasp?

how do i remind myself that
my greatest rival is locked within the mirror,
that the most beautiful of all
bear the heaviest burdens,
though they carry the lightest hearts?

after all is said and done,
i must continually ask my reflection:
how will the angels embrace me in the end?
how will my soul find its final destination?

some of us are blessed with blessings
some of us are cursed with them

The nature of "life" is that we transition from one womb, only to enter another. We leave the comfort of our mother's womb, only to enter the confines of the *dunya* (worldly life). Then eventually, we will depart from the earthly realm yet again, to enter the embrace of the grave.

What a loyal companion *sincerity* is. It benefits you in the *dunya* (worldly life), even before it elevates your status in the hereafter.

the human heart has a capacity—

relinquish control

love is never lost—

designate it to The Divine

detach yourself from the beloved—

attach yourself to your Creator

Forgiveness is a lofty goal that only those who sacrifice an aspect of their *nafs* (soul) can achieve. Is every injustice worthy of forgiveness? Is every perpetrator deserving of it? Most likely not. But we do it for our Selves. We do it for our freedom. We do it for our hereafter. We do it for our Lord.

I have never seen a more peaceful act of revolution
than praying. It is powerful, *yet gentle.*

If you are finding that you do not *feel* anything during your *ibaada*[12]—try again, with more focus.

---

12. "*Ibaada*" is an Arabic term that translates to "worship" or "devotion" in English. In an Islamic context, it refers to acts of worship and obedience to Allah (swt). *Ibaada* encompasses a wide range of actions and attitudes, including ritualistic acts such as prayers (*salah*), fasting (*sawm*), charity (*zakat*), and pilgrimage to Makkah (*hajj*). However, it also extends beyond formal rituals to encompass the entirety of a Muslim's life, emphasizing sincerity, submission, and obedience to the will of Allah (swt) in all aspects of daily living.

Which heart amongst us would not find peace in knowing that its final destination will be decided by *Al-Rahmaan* (The Most Merciful)?

Angels, like mathematicians, meticulously calculate deeds and misdeeds with precise numbers. However, Allah's (swt) mercy transcends everything, shattering *all* algorithms.

expect to be betrayed
by what you betrayed with

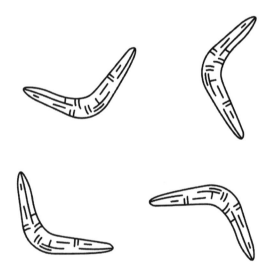

It is not your place to try to fix or heal someone else's problems. Each individual has their own path to traverse and their own lessons to learn. If someone is not ready to change or confront their issues, it is not *your* job to try to force them to. Honor their journey and permit them to pursue the lessons that Allah (swt) has in store for them. It may be difficult to watch from the sidelines, but it is important to trust in Allah's (swt) plan—remember that He is *Al-Hakeem* (The Most Wise).

when the eyes no longer witness
and the soul ceases to feel
when the heart no longer sees
and the mind no longer ponders,
the seals are set—the chains locked tight
yet the keys remain within our palms,
burning through like hot coals[13].

no one said faith would be easy—
yet somehow i thought
i could cruise through it—
but five prayers a day became mere motions.
i lost the essence of conversating with my Creator
and *wudoo*[14] became autopilot—a ritual cleanse.

i have taken this faith for granted.

i have never encountered a religion where God
declared the uniqueness of every fingertip,
every genome, far beyond what science can fathom
—breathless, panting—
it tries to catch up to Divine revelation.

i have taken this faith for granted.

in the desert of Bedouins, time was measured
wisely—
sands flowing through hourglass hands.
recognizing a woman's power is in her compassion,
embracing a man's power is in his vulnerability.

i have taken this faith for granted.

i was taught to prostrate anywhere on this earth—
as long as it is clean.
why then do i doubt that Allah can hear
the ache within my bruised and battered heart—
even when it is too shattered for words,
spilling into heartfelt supplication?

i bear witness that there is no God, *except* Allah—
now i must stand resolute as a servant of The Most
High.

---

13. Anas ibn Malik reported: The Messenger of Allah (pbuh) said, "A time of patience will come to people in which adhering to one's religion is like grasping a hot coal" (Tirmidhi 2260). It signifies that there will be times of difficulty when holding onto one's faith will be challenging and painful, akin to holding a burning coal. It emphasizes the importance of patience and perseverance in maintaining one's faith during trying times.

14. "*Wudoo*" is an Arabic term in Islam that refers to the ritual purification performed before prayer. It involves washing specific parts of the body, such as the hands, face, and feet, as a form of spiritual cleansing.

how many times must my soul shatter
before it returns to its Creator?

The thing about envy is that it cannot remain hidden for long. It cannot hide from the one who envies, nor from the one who is envied. It is more common to find that envy secretly consumes the one who harbors evil intentions in their heart, but in some cases, it can be sensed even by the one who is envied.

It cannot be concealed forever.

Anything that sits and festers in the heart for a lengthy time will eventually surface through the speech, or the actions. It will reveal itself. And when it rears its ugly head, take heed of the signs and do not assume that the one who envies will ever change just by default of your goodwill. Indeed, the one who wishes destruction upon another human being cannot be satiated except by the removal of the blessings of the envied one. May Allah (swt) protect those whom He has endowed His blessings upon. And may He guide those who envy others' blessings. *Ameen.*

Some people's bodies may reside in opulent castles—
but their hearts remain confined within the dungeons
of life's trials and tribulations. For the one who reflects
often on death and life knows that external circumstances or worldly possessions should not be the sole
focus in our life. Rather, the state of one's heart and
spiritual well-being is of the *greatest* importance.

If Allah (swt) says that there will be no evil speech, such as gossiping or backbiting in *Jannah* (paradise), what makes you think that you will get there if you are engaging in that kind of behavior now?

Do not underestimate the power and influence of music on your heart. The heart's natural rhythm can be disrupted by music and its captivating sound. It can divert you from achieving its purpose. Guard your heart—as if your life depended on it.

sometimes we block our own blessings

The prevalence of the "I said what I said" culture in our society highlights a prevalent issue: the notion that merely speaking one's mind is enough. However, in many instances, what often goes unnoticed is how these words are delivered. In Islam, the way we communicate is of utmost importance, as the Prophet Muhammad (pbuh) emphasized the significance of choosing our words wisely and speaking with kindness and respect. This encompasses not only what is said but also *how* it is said, as it reflects on a person's sincerity and intention.

the longevity of your success
is dependent on your sincerity

let the ego

subdue

its cravings

and find satiation

in the morgue

of its appetites.

The more that you achieve—or acquire of the *dunya* (worldly life), the more unfulfilling you will find it to be. *True happiness and contentment can only be found in a developing a deeper connection with Allah (swt).*

"The *dunya* (worldly life) is like a shadow. If you try to catch it, you will never be able to do so. If you turn your back toward it, it has no choice but to follow you."

—*Ibn al-Qayyim*

they say all new things
carry a certain smell—
    it enters through the nose
    and it sits in the soul.
you see, the thing about luxury is that
even if it does not make you sin—
    it will distract you from the
    blessed remembrance
    it will make you forget
    to be grateful
    while still enjoying the favors.
but you must check on your heart
    knock on its walls to see
    how strong do they stand?
    how fortified are they
    in the midst of the war?
    do they crumble?
    are they sturdy
    like castles protecting all
    the flaws *shaytaan* could use
    if he had the access?

keep your eyes on the prize, my sister.

The *wrong* type of success can feel lonely.

Some individuals excel through the actions of their body:
they pray more, fast more, and make more dua.

Others excel through the actions of their heart:
they do not harbor envy toward those with "more" than
them, they think positive thoughts about Allah (swt),
and they readily forgive

Which of these do *you* excel in?

the ego: tame it with sincerity
whip it down with softness
let it fertilize the soil—
the very dust from
which you were created.

A talent is a gift from God. What you choose to do with it is what determines whether it becomes a blessing or a curse.

If you seek to remain protected when people come for you in this cancel culture, then do your utmost to preserve the honor and dignity of others at all times—whether you like them or not.

The Prophet Muhammad (pbuh) wisely told us, "Whoever believes in Allah (swt) and the Last Day, let him speak good or remain silent." Upholding the principle of "*israf*" (avoiding excess) in speech, even in the face of adversity, becomes a shield in the realm of cancel culture. By preserving the sanctity of others, you carve a path to safeguard your own standing.

when i write, i must ask myself:
what do you love?
what compels your palms
to rise in supplication?
what lowers your forehead to bow
in the pursuit of forgiveness
for every small sin committed
—*still committing.*
i will tell you. it is the devotion to a word
stronger than anything i've ever known:
Laa ilaaha illallah.

You are unique. And your purpose is intertwined with what brings fulfillment to your heart. Seek inspiration—*absolutely*. But also, be original. Because your calling to serve Allah (swt) is intricately linked to what sets you apart.

when sorrow finds
itself stuck in your throat
—*like a coarse piece of bread*—
not fully chewed, not yet digested,
it just proliferates like a biblical loaf
from the hand of prophet.

your heart must accept the test:
neither an entire earth nor its inhabitants
could prevent a calamity
that was written for you.
so come *willingly*
or *unwillingly*—
you will arrive.

the pens have been lifted,
the ink is dry.

each trial issues its blow:
but i'd rather this life test me
before *Munkar* and *Nakeeer*[15]
whom by design, possess no mercy.
is this not enough to send an avalanche
of shivers through any spine
that fears its Lord as it should?
the same spine that shall bend
when His Shin[16] reveals itself
and the self-reproaching soul
reminisces over why
it was so obstinate
in transgression.

---

15. *Munkar and Nakeer:* There will be two angels whose task it is to question the deceased once they are placed in their grave. Their description is that they are black and blue in appearance, and one is called al-Munkar and the other is called al-Nakeer. They will ask the following three questions: Who is your Lord? What is your religion? Who is this man (Prophet Muhammad (pbuh)) who was sent among you?

16. Muslims believe that Allah (swt) will reveal His noble Shin on the Day of Judgment, and every believer, male and female, will prostrate to Him. Regarding the hypocrites who would ostentatiously prostrate to Allah (swt) in the worldly life merely to be seen by others, they will find themselves unable to prostrate in the hereafter as their backs will be fused into a single vertebra. This consequence befalls them because their prostrations in the worldly life lacked sincerity towards Allah (swt). It is obligatory to affirm this attribute for Allah (swt) without asking "how," without drawing resemblances or similitudes, and without stripping it of its true meaning.

Allah (swt) does not break His promises. Therefore, if we do not receive what He has assured us, the question arises: *which party has breached the covenant?*

Most people marvel at the success of others.

People may assume that your achievements are a result of circumstance—that somehow you were given a hand up. That you are "privileged" and by default did not have to toil so hard for what you have. The truth is, each and every one of us has been gifted with something unique from Allah (swt)—this is how you will discover your "privilege." Recognize and be grateful for the blessings you have been granted. If tapping into them seems challenging, take a moment to reflect on your strengths and unique characteristics—you will undoubtedly find that Allah (swt) has bestowed upon you the tools to overcome adversity. Embrace your strengths, trust in Allah's (swt) plan, and persevere with the knowledge that your unique qualities are Divinely crafted to navigate the path set before you.

the ego

the ego

the ego

Being in a position of leadership also means being in a position of influence. In Islam, embracing discomfort in leadership could be a sign of spiritual growth. Leadership should encourage you to continuously improve *yourself*. It also means you have to devote yourself to serving others—recognizing that true worth is derived not only from your personal accomplishments but also from the positive impact you have on your community. Have no doubt that this always comes full circle—when you serve others, you also serve yourself.

i have two eyes—
one to look within
and one to peer outwardly.

the sand dunes
within the hourglass
sink.
time elapses,
moving into oblivion.
the human mind
thinks
that its vessel
will contain it for eternity,
but the grave
links
life and a hereafter.
direct your gaze to a sky
full of glistening
starry jewels.
blink
and your eyesight
will return to you humbled.
as the universe expands—
the backbone of a man
shrinks.

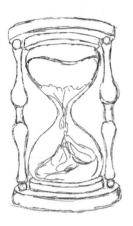

The inherent nature of human beings means that we often feel uneasy and impatient when confronted with things that are beyond our understanding. In the Quran, there is a dialogue between Khidr (as) and Musa (as) that emphasizes the challenge of exercising patience in the face of the unknown[17]. Khidr (as) questions Musa (as) about his ability to be patient in situations where the depth of knowledge is not fully grasped. This Divine reminder should encourage us to reflect on the limitations of our understanding—as well as the importance of cultivating patience when faced with the mysteries of life.

---

17. The story of Khidr (as) and Musa (as) is recounted in the Quran in Surah Al-Kahf (18:65–82). In the narrative, Prophet Musa (Moses) meets a mysterious and knowledgeable figure named Khidr. Musa (as) asks to accompany Khidr (as) and learn from him, to which Khidr (as) agrees, but with the condition that Musa does not question his actions. The conditions set by Khidr (as) not to question his actions play a crucial role in conveying profound spiritual lessons. Khidr's (as) insistence on Musa's (as) compliance with this condition serves as a symbolic representation of the limitations of human understanding when it comes to comprehending the Divine plan.

During their journey, Khidr (as) performs three seemingly perplexing actions: damaging a boat, killing a young man, and repairing a wall in a town that refused to offer them hospitality. Musa (as), unable to restrain himself, questions these actions, and each time Khidr (as) provides a deeper, often hidden, wisdom behind his actions.

This story serves as a reminder that sometimes events unfold in ways that may seem contradictory to our understanding. Khidr's (as) actions, when explained, reveal hidden dimensions of wisdom that highlight the intricate workings of the Divine plan. The story encourages believers to embrace patience, humility, and trust in Allah (swt), even in the face of uncertainty or events that challenge their understanding.

Just because you may not like a *truth* does not inherently change the reality of that truth. Rather than getting caught up in external circumstances we cannot change, we can adapt our responses instead. It is this flexibility and resilience in the face of change that becomes the cornerstone of not just survival—but of spiritual growth too.

If an increase in worship, or the acquisition of knowledge leads to arrogance—there is something deficient in the heart. Instead, both of these virtuous deeds should instill humbleness in the body and soul. *Good deeds should make the heart more submissive to Allah (swt).* And they should make the tongue full of locks so that it must strive hard to unchain itself in a moment of rage or weakness. If the tongue is loose, and the heart considers itself better than others, it trudges down a dark path.

Sometimes the deed that matters the most
is the one you *almost* did not do.

i used to witness children laughing
playing tag on the sun-flooded
tiles of my forecourt
used to see them grow an inch each year
until they had *nikahs*[18] and *aqeeqahs*[19] of their own
now i witness mostly *janaza*[20] prayers
yes—there is a musk that I can smell within the
folds of shrouds.

but I miss the *misk*[21] i'd smell on fridays the most.

muhammad with his *miswaak*[22] brushing back and
forth like a pendulum, laughing away at ali's jokes.

and khadijah always making the babies coo and
laugh

my walls witness many things
but these bricks become colder
as my foundations become older
and there is nobody inside me making *tawbah*[23],
no more foot to foot—
shoulder to shoulder.

my domes painted with *tasbeeh*[24]
would shelter the regular worshipping servant,
the friday-only attendee, the prayer of *taraweeh*[25],

the sinner who left and returned with tears in his
eyes and repentance in his palms

she who was burdened with the heaviness of the
world, dropped it off her chest as she lowered herself in
sujood[26].

the seeker of tranquility hidden in the last third of
the night

attaining success before finding the *fajr*[27] light.

my dome covered many things

it covered the sins of each believer—seeking refuge
from *riba*[28] and *zina*[29], the one who loves her mother,
her mother, her mother, and then her father[30]

i miss the *mu'atthin*[31]
bringing life to the minarets,
flooding each crack and crevice with the gracious call.
now i hear only the caretaker from time to time,
with his brush sweeping away
the dust above each Quran
untouched for one long and lonely year.
i think about my guests every day,
but do they think about me?

---

18. *"Nikah"* is the Arabic word for an Islamic marriage, a sacred contract between a man and a woman.

19. An *"aqeeqah"* is an Islamic tradition involving the ritual sacrifice of an animal, typically a sheep or goat, as a symbol of gratitude and celebration for the birth of a child.

20. *"Janaza"* refers to the Islamic funeral prayer or the funeral procession itself, marking the ritualistic process of burying a deceased person in accordance with Islamic traditions.

21. *"Misk"* is an Arabic word that translates to "musk" in English.

22. "*Miswak*" is a teeth-cleaning twig, often from the Salvadora persica tree, used for oral hygiene in many Islamic cultures as part of a tradition endorsed by Prophet Muhammad (pbuh).

23. "*Tawba*h" in Islamic terminology, refers to repentance—a sincere and remorseful turning away from sins and a commitment to righteous behavior after seeking forgiveness from Allah (swt).

24. "*Tasbeeh*" refers to the act of glorifying and praising Allah (swt) by reciting repetitive phrases as a form of remembrance and devotion in Islam.

25. "*Taraweeh*" is a special nightly prayer performed during the month of Ramadan in Islam, involving the recitation of long portions of the Quran, usually in congregation at the mosque.

26. "*Sujood*" refers to the act of prostration during prayer, where a Muslim bows down and places their forehead, nose, palms, knees, and toes on the ground as a symbol of humility and submission to Allah (swt).

27. "*Fajr*" is one of the five daily prayers; it is performed before sunrise.

28. "*Riba*" in Islamic finance, refers to the prohibition of usury or unjust enrichment through interest, emphasizing fair and equitable financial transactions.

29. "*Zina*" refers to the prohibited act of illicit sexual relations or adultery, which is considered a major sin in Islam.

30. Abu Huraira reported: A man asked the Messenger of Allah (pbuh), "Who is most deserving of my good company?" The Prophet (pbuh) said, "Your mother." The man asked, "Then who?" The Prophet (pbuh) said "Your mother." The man asked again, "Then who?" The Prophet (pbuh) said, "Your mother." The man asked again, "Then who?" The Prophet (pbuh) said, "Your father." (Bukhari 5971)

31. The "*mu'atthin*" is the person appointed to call the *adhan* (Islamic call to prayer) from the minaret of a mosque.

rabbi inni limaa anzalta ilayya min khayrin faqeer

My Lord! Truly, I am in need of whatever
good that You bestow on me!

(The Quran, 28:24)

remember the words of Musa after fleeing Egypt
—a refugee—
sitting underneath a tree
he invoked His Lord

so when the tyrant brings you to your knees—
be it an abuser, a psychological intruder,
a disobedient child, a toxic spouse—
then use this prayer to seek assistance
from your Lord

good and bad
placed on the scales—
my
soul
hangs
in
the
balance

where will i go? where will i go?
where will i go?

then i remember the words of my Messenger (pbuh):

"When Allah completed the creation, He wrote in His
book, upon the Throne: Verily, My mercy prevails
over My wrath[32]."

---

32. On the authority of Abu Hurayrah (as), who said that the Messenger of
Allah (pbuh) said: When Allah (swt) decreed the Creation, He pledged Himself
by writing in His book, which is laid down with Him: "My mercy prevails over
My wrath." (Hadith Qudsi 1)

Imagine if the specific lesson for *you* in the story of Yusuf (as) was *not* about maintaining chastity when seduced into committing sin. Rather, it was a caution against harboring envy, akin to the brothers of Yusuf (as).

the future holds tests
the past holds lessons

We should not be so hasty to equate *loss* with Divine punishment. Nor should *gain* be understood solely as a measure of Allah's (swt) favor on us. Islam teaches that Allah's (swt) wisdom transcends our immediate understanding, and what may appear as a setback, could actually be a blessing, a test—or a means of purification.

confidence is easily
mistaken for arrogance
by those who have
yet to master it

Eloquence is not the only trait required for leadership. In fact, the bewitching power of articulation is often misused by those with corrupt intentions. So, if you find yourself struggling to express your thoughts, or stumbling on your words—despite your sincerity, then remember that *true* wisdom often resides in speaking less. A compelling example is Prophet Musa (as), who, despite facing a speech impediment, exemplified profound leadership.

be *soft*, be strong

be kind to your Self
before all else

oh Father
of the prophets, *Ibraheem*[33].
close companion
of Allah—*Khalilullah*[34]—
tell me how it is to walk
alone as an *ummah*?
to be cast into a fire
by your own father?
to be rejected by your tribe
when you were only a boy?

i saw your footprint in Makkah.

your father constructed idols
but you obliterated them
and you built the *ka'bah*
with *your* righteous son.

man of profound vision.

what amazes me the *most*
is knowing that my Prophet Muhammad (pbuh)
had a face that looked just like yours.

---

33. In Islam, the Prophet Ibrahim ("*Ibraheem*" in Arabic, and "Abraham" in English) is revered as a key figure and patriarch. Known for his unwavering faith and submission to Allah (swt), Ibrahim (as) is recognized as one of the greatest prophets. His life story, encompassing trials such as the construction of the *Ka'bah* and the willingness to sacrifice his son Isma'eel (as) in obedience to Allah's (swt) command, serves as a profound example of devotion, resilience, and trust in God's plan.

34. The title *Khalilullah* is often used to describe Prophet Ibrahim (as), meaning "Friend of God." This name reflects the closeness and intimacy that Ibrahim (as) had with the Allah (swt) in the Islamic tradition.

didn't you know that *giving*
does not *take* anything away from you?
look at the sun: it gives light in the day,
only for the moon to return it at night.

be pious

Do not attach yourself to people in the hope that you will receive something from them. Ask *only* of your Lord, and undoubtedly, He will bring the people—in unprecedented ways—as an answer to your prayer.

when all else abandons you,
know that if you have Allah (swt)
—you have *everything*.

If the thing that differentiates you from others is worldly, you have already *lost*. However, if what distinguishes you from others is your *emaan* (faith), then you possess the real treasure.

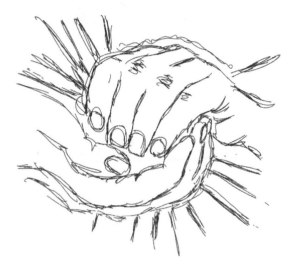

As long as you make pleasing Allah (swt) your biggest concern, He will continue strengthening you on your path.

Nothing is ever lost in helping someone in need. In fact, *more is gained.* The Prophet Muhammad (pbuh) said:

"And to walk with a brother to meet his needs is dearer to me than observing i'tikaaf [35] in this mosque—meaning the mosque of Madinah—for a month."

(Tabaraani 12:453)

---

35. *"I'tikaf"* is a practice in Islam where a Muslim secludes oneself in the mosque with the intention of dedicating time to worship and spiritual activities. This voluntary act is usually performed in the last ten days of Ramadan, the holy month of fasting. The word *"i'tikaf"* is derived from the Arabic root *'a-kh-f,* which means "to adhere" or "to stick."

when you remember someone
in a moment of difficulty,
they will remember you
for a *lifetime*.

"And what is the reward of goodness, but goodness."
(The Quran, 55:60)

What you sow today will bear fruit tomorrow. And the quality of the harvest is equivalent to the effort invested. However, when connected to spiritual mission, you will find that your efforts are rewarded exponentially—this is how Allah (swt) rewards those who do good for *His* sake.

though i know not which deed will yield
the sweetest fruit—i still scatter the seeds.
i am guided by the belief that every effort
is witnessed by Allah (swt).
i *place my trust in Him.*

did you think that when you said
"*laa ilaaha ilAllah*"[36]
that your life would get easier?
indeed, this is when
the *real* test of your faith begins.

---

36. "*Laa ilaha illallah*" is a fundamental declaration in Islam, known as the *shahada*. It translates to "there is no god but Allah" in English. This phrase encapsulates the central tenet of Islamic monotheism: affirming the belief in the oneness of Allah (swt) and rejecting any partners or deities. The *shahada* is a concise expression of a Muslim's faith, and its utterance is a declaration of one's conversion to Islam.

the corners of this parched mouth
become moist with remembrance.
tears water the prayer rug
as the tug of war plays out
between the *nafs* and clay—
i call this home.

but what if this soul is home
and this body is the *temporary* abode?
what if this sin is like a comb that
scrapes faith off the heart
like cream off the top of milk?

the manifestation
of revelation
in a Muslim
is reflected in their
mannerisms

seek virtue *not*
in the outward appearance
but in the depths
of the inner world—
especially when deciding
on a spouse

the heart—master of the ship
cautiously whips limbs
like slaves.
they will submit
to what they are
commanded to do—
choose wisely

i asked for ease

my chest became open

i asked for peace

my burden became light

i asked for the way

the Qur'an gave me direction

i was lost along the way

my path became illuminated

the path to peace
is the distance between
wudoo[37] to *sajda*[38].
the truth witnessed in the twilight
—affirmed at the breaking of dawn—
it slits the ego
into soul and flesh
and is built back up again
by the bones of belief.
Allahu Akbar[39]—I begin.

37. "*Wudoo*" is the Arabic word for "ablution" in English. It is a ritual purification in Islam involving the washing of specific parts of the body before certain acts of worship, such as prayer and touching the Quran. The process includes washing the hands, mouth, nose, face, arms up to the elbows, wiping the head, and washing the feet. *Wudoo* is performed with the intention of seeking purification and spiritual readiness. It is considered an essential prerequisite for the validity of certain religious activities in Islam. The practice symbolizes both physical and spiritual cleanliness, fostering a state of purity for engaging in acts of devotion.

38. "*Sajda*" is an Arabic term in Islam that translates to "prostration" or "bowing down." It refers to the act of placing the forehead, nose, both palms, both knees, and the toes of both feet on the ground during the Islamic prayer *(salah)*. "*Sajda*" is a crucial component of the prayer ritual and symbolizes complete submission and humility before Allah (swt). The position of "*sajda*" is considered a moment of intense spiritual connection and surrender, signifying the servant's devotion and acknowledgment of the greatness of the Creator. It is a physical manifestation of humility, gratitude, and reverence in the worshiper's relationship with Allah (swt).

39. "*Allahu Akbar*" (in Arabic) translates to "Allah is the Greatest" in English. This phrase is a fundamental and frequently used expression in Islam. "*Allahu Akbar*" is recited in various contexts, such as during the call to prayer *(adhan)*, in moments of joy and distress, and during various rituals and prayers. It serves as a reminder of the centrality of Allah's (swt) greatness in the life and faith of a Muslim.

Glory be
to The One who
simply said "Be"
and it was!

True self-sufficiency is not attained by those who do not depend on anyone. Rather, they are the ones who rely on Allah (swt) *alone*. Thus, He gifts them a unique sense of independence that exudes from within.

Just because you love a person does not guarantee that they will love you back. *Except your Creator*: walk to Him, and He will run to you. Meet Him with an earth full of sin, and He will welcome you with boundless forgiveness[40].

---

40. Abu Dharr reported: The Messenger of Allah, (pbuh), said, "Allah Almighty says: Whoever comes with a good deed will have the reward of ten like it and even more. Whoever comes with an evil deed will be recompensed for one evil deed like it or he will be forgiven. Whoever draws close to Me by the length of a hand, I will draw close to him by the length of an arm. Whoever draws close to Me the by length of an arm, I will draw close to him by the length of a fathom. Whoever comes to Me walking, I will come to him running. Whoever meets Me with enough sins to fill the earth, not associating any partners with Me, I will meet him with as much forgiveness." (Muslim 2687)

how can I ask the sun for shade?
how can I ask the shadow for originality?
how can I ask my heart to betray itself?
how can I worship anything
except the One who created?

The same staff that Prophet Musa (as) used to part the waters into dry paths is the same one that channels Divine blessings. This is a powerful reminder that miracles flow through the ordinary when guided by true faith.

Do you thank others for their support or assistance in your time of need? If you have not yet done so, then you have not truly thanked Allah (swt). True success is forbidden from the one who does not show gratitude—and gratitude is a *verb*.

At times, we may find ourselves unprepared to receive what is truly best for us. Therefore, as we beseech Allah (swt) for goodness in our lives, let us also implore Him to open our hearts to *receive* His blessings, aligning our souls with His divine wisdom and readiness to accept His kindness.

To be *strange* when we take a path in pursuit of Allah's (swt) pleasure is often romanticized. What they don't tell you about is the reality of sacrifice, pain, and rejection that accompanies this journey. But all of that is buffered by the sweetness of faith—and it is not for the faint of heart.

When I think of Prophet Ibrahim (as), and how he was the only believer on this earth, at one point, I wonder what he felt in that moment—loneliness, rejection, betrayal ...

These emotions often form the essence of our existence when we choose the road less traveled for the sake of Allah (swt). We may appear peculiar as the only one in our friend's group who pauses in the street to pray. We might be perceived as the oddball for abstaining from a casual puff while everyone around us indulges in smoking.

Despite this, *embrace* your strangeness—just like the Prophet Ibrahim (as).

the speech between the eyes
    will eventually cease
the language of hearts
    whispers into eternity
this world tries to convince you of its value
    through seduction and external decoration
but the most precious things are those
    most difficult to acquire
will you pick an instant gratification
    over a lasting pleasure?
the choice is your own
    the suffering—your own

clasp onto *laa ilaaha illAllah*
—even if you are struggling to live by it—
do not lose hope in such
a forgiving Lord.

be *soft*, be strong

Little do we know that we are not closest to Him in the exploration of the stars, but in the lowest and most humbled position—in prostration.

keep your tongue moving
around the labyrinth
of the mouth's cave.
let it rise in power,
then lower in humility
—unshackle it to praise Him.

i witness a spectacle of swords
clashing against the backdrop
of a setting horizon.
yet, their fury cannot surpass
the beauty of God—*Al-Jameel*[41]

41. Allah's (swt) name *"Al-Jameel"* serves as a reminder for believers to acknowledge and appreciate the inherent beauty in Allah's (swt) creation. It also encourages them to aspire to moral and spiritual beauty in their own lives. This name
underscores the concept that Allah's (swt) attributes are flawless, making Him
the epitome of beauty in every sense.

I am already at war with myself—
do not invite me to your battlefield.

Do not be fooled by the impact that toxic energy can have on you. Toxic individuals are about as abundant as the air that we breathe. But remember, *you* are in control of who—or what—you allow into your life. Safeguard your heart because it is the most important part of your body and your soul. Allowing others or yourself to corrupt it is akin to permitting your entire being to be tainted by poison.

But what is the antidote? Cultivate emotional and spiritual awareness of your thoughts, as they are the seeds that will inevitably sprout into actions. Once you have mastered your mind, no negativity will be able to permeate your core. Instead, such energy enters, then departs—but it never overstays its welcome.

beauty holds the eyes captive—
but piety crowns the heart.

be *soft*

Allah (swt) loves you. Even in those moments when you do not love yourself. When you cannot find an inch of beauty in your form. When you are burdened with the regret of your sins. When you are laden with the guilt of falling short despite knowing better—His love remains consistent. In repentance, you will find that He was always there for you—loving, forgiving, and kind.

sometimes
they do not seek your strength—
they seek your *soft*.

let the *hijab* unveil its layers to reveal
to the worthy hand, and the purest heart,
the beauty that radiates beneath it—
like an oyster prized from its shell

the secret glow on the face of a woman of faith
cannot be achieved by makeup—it is through
tahajjud[42]:
in the velvet darkness
—when the world slumbers—
her vigilant lone soul awakes
the moon is a witness
the stars silently applaud her
as she prostrates in solitude
embracing the sacred laws of success

oh, the beauty of *tahajjud*!
when the world is still—
a sacred dialogue
where all ills and secrets are spilled—
her palms raised high
like fragrant petals
as if she is saying to her Lord:
here are my burdens,
i entrust them to you

this is the sacred rendezvous with The Divine,
it adds nothing but beauty
to her face when she rises
from beneath the canopy
of the night

---

42. The *Tahajjud* prayer holds special significance in Islam, and it is encouraged by various hadith (sayings and actions of Prophet Muhammad (pbuh)) One notable hadith emphasizes the virtues of *Tahajjud*:

Narrated by Abu Huraira, the Prophet Muhammad (pbuh) said: "In the last third of every night, our Lord, The Blessed, The Superior, descends to the nearest heaven and says: 'Is there anyone to invoke Me, that I may respond to his invocation? Is there anyone to ask Me, so that I may grant him his request? Is there anyone seeking My forgiveness, so that I may forgive him?'" (Bukhari 1145)

May Allah (swt) bless those people who believe in your potential before you have achieved any of your dreams. *They are rare*. Most people support you only *after* witnessing your aspirations manifested. This kind of devotion reminds me of Khadijah[43] (as), who did not once question the Prophet (pbuh) when he came with the message of truth. She loved him before prophethood, and steadfastly stood by him throughout it.

---

43. Khadijah Bint Khuwaylid, a prominent figure in Islamic history, was the first wife of Prophet Muhammad (pbuh). Born into a noble and affluent family in Makkah, Khadijah (as) became known for her intelligence, compassion, and strong character. She was a highly successful businesswoman, managing her own trade caravan business.

Prophet Muhammad (pbuh) worked for Khadijah (as) as a merchant, overseeing her trade caravans. His honesty, integrity, and noble qualities left a deep impression on Khadijah (as). Recognizing his virtues, she proposed to him through a close friend, and they were married. This union marked the beginning of a supportive and loving partnership.

Together, Khadijah (as) and Prophet Muhammad (pbuh) had several children, including two sons, Al-Qasim and Abdullah, and four daughters, Zainab, Fatima, Ruqayya, and Umm Kulthoom. Khadijah (as) played a pivotal role in the early years of Prophet Muhammad's (pbuh) prophethood, offering both emotional and financial support.

Tragically, Khadijah (as) passed away in 619 CE, before the Prophet's migration to Medina. Despite her physical absence, her memory lived on, and Prophet Muhammad (pbuh) spoke of her with enduring love and respect. Khadijah's (as) contributions to the early Muslim community and her unwavering support for the Prophet (pbuh) solidify her esteemed place in Islamic history.

He hears you—
even in your silence.

Do not *ever* stay in a place where
you have to negotiate your worth.

Who must qualify you so that your existence matters? How many more rooms must you be silent in before you can release your true Self? How many more times must you muffle the truth for fear of offending others' egos?

who taught you to hate yourself?
to hate the hue of your soul
or the bridge of your nose?
who taught you that beauty
was the opposite of *you?*
was every crease that the years
pressed like iron into your skin
after every kin
unlearned their mother tongue
and whipped it straight to speak
the queen's english.
who taught you to feel shame
in the aroma of your homeland cuisine?
it will stick to your clothes
like the cement that clenches to each brick—
it holds a house in you—no, *a home*.

Do not allow others to make you feel guilty when you prioritize that which aligns most with your personal and spiritual values. The unquestionable reality of life is that we are only here for a limited time, and so we must continually ask ourselves "what is *most* meaningful to me?"

Some people do not realize that if you are *sincere*,
their validation matters very little.

Maybe you are a person who does not wear their heart on their sleeve for the vultures of the world to rip apart? Rather, you keep your heart tucked deep inside your chest, and you are reserved in who you allow to enter it. There is nothing wrong with wanting to protect yourself in this way. After all, we come alone into this world, we leave alone, and then we meet Allah (swt) alone. But don't let this ever make you afraid of taking a leap of faith and stepping out of your comfort zone. You might find your greatest achievements are born in these moments.

be *soft*, be strong

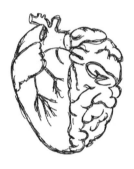

just like the brain,
the heart has a memory

The next time someone acts entitled and bombards you with questions about your life, before you respond, ask yourself the following: *what has this person demonstrated to earn the privilege of accessing information about me?* This will help you appreciate that not everyone you encounter deserves insight into your personal life.

Access to you is a privilege. This does not make you arrogant. It simply makes you conscious. Purposeful. *Intentional*.

I used to think, "Is this worth my time?" But now, I contemplate, "Is this worth my *energy*?"

There are some kinds of *tired* that sleep cannot alleviate; a type of weariness that is etched into the soul—a fatigue that lingers even after sleep. It is a weariness not born of physical exertion, but of navigating the complexities of existence—the weight of the *dunya*, and the silent battles fought within. Similar to caring for your body, make sure your soul receives the rest it deserves.

Be gentle with yourself for the mistakes you made in the past. If your inner voice is too loud and critical of those shortcomings—despite your remorse, you are doing your soul a disservice. Be particularly kind to yourself in those moments by recalling that Allah (swt) is *Al-Wadood*, The Most Loving. And remember, kindness to the world can only be shared once you have extended it to yourself first.

sometimes I hurt
sometimes I heal

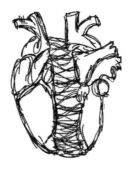

what is this broken and bruised
pound of flesh
that Allah (swt) placed to rest
in the center of my chest?

the blood courses forward,
and it has no option but to leave—
only to return renewed and purified
with every *wudoo* and *sujood*

if your love for Him
could drown an ocean,
or turn a mountain to dust,
or stop the beaming sun
in its course, maybe then
you would realize His love
for you is even greater

Be careful with what you choose to love,
for that is where you will be tested.

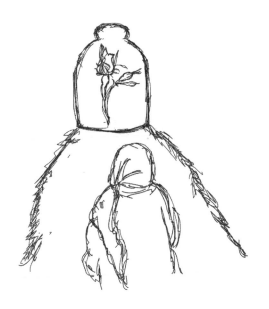

It is not *love* that inflicts pain, but the misguided *attachment* to people and to fleeting pursuits. To find true happiness, redirect the core of your affection to Allah (swt)—The Everlasting. In your love for Him, you will find love for everything else. More importantly, you will also find the eternal peace that your heart longs for.

Those who stray the farthest, return the strongest. So never judge a person by where they are, but by how far they have come.

each person possesses
a redeeming quality
and every human
bears a fatal flaw
What are yours?

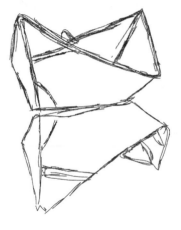

do not attach yourself to things—*things can easily break.*

do not attach yourself to people—*people change.*

do not attach yourself to the world—*the world goes through seasons.*

Do not muffle your intuition. *It is a compass*. It is a Divinely placed way of keeping you attuned to the subtleties that others may overlook. It is a hidden guide tightly bound to spiritual safety and connectedness. Even when your eyes see smiles, something deep within your soul may sense hostility. Pay heed to it.

Wabisah bin Ma'bad (as) reported:

I went to Messenger of Allah (pbuh) and he asked me, "Have you come to inquire about piety?" I replied in the affirmative. Then he said, "Ask your heart regarding it. Piety is that which contents the soul and comforts the heart, and sin is that which causes doubts and perturbs the heart, even if people pronounce it lawful and give you verdicts on such matters again and again." (Ahmad & Ad-Darmi)

This profound advice emphasizes the importance of introspection and consulting one's heart in matters of piety and righteousness.

Those who understand optimism best, are often the ones
who have experienced the depths of depression.

In order for your hands to be in a position to receive Allah's (swt) blessings, sometimes it means that you must first release the things that your hands are still grasping onto.

sometimes I laugh

sometimes I weep

sometimes I wilt

sometimes I grow

sometimes I stay

sometimes I go

always I pray

anger is a sadness
that has not yet
been released
through prayer

Sometimes people are not boasting when they tell you their achievements. Maybe when they were younger, they were never told "I am proud of you."

Do not live out your days with the assumption that tomorrow is guaranteed for you. There is no knowing when The Angel of Death with arrive. So treat each moment as if it were your last: *this might be the last prayer you make*. It might be the last time you get to call your mother and hear her voice. Embrace those moments because life is full of uncertainties—but living with intentionality and purpose will *never* yield regret.

with every new love
your heart expands.
with every loss
you learn what
truly matters.

It is in your vulnerability that you will find your strength. Look at Prophet Musa (as)—he had a speech impediment, but he was called *kalimallah*[44].

---

44. "*Kalimallah*" is an Arabic term that translates to "the one who spoke with Allah (swt)." It is an honorary title given to the Prophet Musa (Moses) in Islam. This designation highlights his unique and intimate communication with Allah (swt), as mentioned in the Quran, where Musa (as) is chosen as a prophet and messenger who directly conversed with the Almighty.

Where can peace truly be found? Could it be within the four walls of this exceptionally decorated and glittering *dunya*? Perhaps it is woven into Aladdin's rug, which cradles my heart five times a day in *salah*[45]? Can it be felt in the coolness of my eyes as they glare in amazement at the marvels of human creation? *Where is peace?* Is it buried beneath the rubble—ravaged by warlords who will soon see this haunting image again in a flashback? *Where can I find it?* Is it preserved within the heart that reminds itself that to Allah (swt) we belong, and to Him we will return? Does it reside in the vastness of the cosmos, or does it rest six feet below? Where can peace be found? *Where?*

45. "*Salah*" is an Arabic term that translates to "prayer" in English. In Islam, *Salah* refers to the ritualistic act of worship, involving specific physical movements and recitations, performed by Muslims facing the *Kaa'bah* in Makkah.

even inside
of rock-hard bones
is the softest marrow

When I was younger, I thought that *possessions* would make me happy—until I acquired them, and they brought me no joy. As I got a little older, I thought that *people* could make me happy—until I was "popular," and most of them disappointed me. Then I thought that only *I* could make myself happy—until I realized that I am full of flaws. Now, I understand that only Allah (swt) can make me happy. He never disappears, never abandons, and never disappoints.

Sometimes all it takes just one person
to believe in you. *Let it be you.*

how do you grieve someone who is not dead?

Navigating the sorrow of losing someone who is still *physically* present but *emotionally* distant—or even *spiritually* disconnected—is deep. *Grieving the vibrant connection that once thrived but has now dwindled away is hard.* But Allah (swt) knows this. He compassionately acknowledges these emotional trials that we will experience within the examples he set for us in the Quran. All the prophets of Allah (swt) experienced this in some capacity—but what helped them through these testing times? It was the remembrance of Allah (swt):

"Verily in the remembrance of Allah do the hearts find peace."

(The Quran, 13:28)

be strong

You will remain weak if you rely solely on *yourself*. But you will discover *true* strength when you place your trust in Allah (swt)—relying on Him *alone*.

Asiyah (as), the wife of the tyrannical Pharaoh, reached a level of excellence in her belief (*ihsaan*[46]). Once Pharaoh came to find out about her belief, and he tortured her in the most unimaginable ways. Despite the intense suffering, her faith remained unshaken, and she achieved the pinnacle of success because of her righteousness. Surely through her inspiring story we find that a "happy" marriage is not necessarily what determines our "success"—contrary to what the social status quo might suggest.

To those who are single, widowed, divorced, or currently facing relationship challenges, know that there is a profound wisdom behind these circumstances—Allah (swt) sees and hears all. And He puts you through these trials in the hopes that it will ultimately bring you closer to Him.

---

46. "*Ihsaan*" is an Arabic term in Islam that translates to "excellence" or "perfection" in English. It represents the highest degree of faith in Islam. The concept is encapsulated in the famous hadith of Jibreel, where the Angel Jibreel (as) asked Prophet Muhammad (pbuh) about *islam, iman, and ihsaan*, with the Prophet (pbuh) describing *ihsaan* as worshiping Allah (swt) as if one sees Him (and if not, then knowing that He sees you).

Do you know the power that is awoken in a woman who is told that covering her body must not have been *her* choice? She is told that a man *must* have commanded her to do it. As if a hefty decision to cover her body could *only* have been made by a man?

As women, we receive many messages from the society that we live in: Your job is to be pretty. You *must* be seen but not heard. You *must* preserve your youth. You *must* make it your life's goal to find a man. And the list goes on. Well, what if all a woman wants is to serve Allah (swt)? To live with *deep* purpose. To work on big dreams. To raise a loving family. To nurture the next generation. Believing women—do not let society dictate to you your value based on the superficial. Pursue what you desire with purpose, and remember, the end goal is to seek Allah's (swt) pleasure—not that of people.

Didn't you know that the moon is *always* present—even in the morning light? But its beauty is not fully witnessed until it is surrounded by darkness. Similarly, it is only when a trial befalls a believer that this *true* faith is revealed. Testing times distinguish real gold from fool's gold.

To my Muslim sister who *chooses* to wear modest clothing in the sweltering heat: *Your struggle does not go unseen.* Allah (swt) knows that you are persevering to cover your body for His sake—especially when everyone around you might be stripping down. You may feel strange wearing longer clothing. You may get comments like *"aren't you hot in that?"* Persevere despite this. Allah (swt) sees your struggle, and trust me, His paradise is worth it.

rise. like a Messiah who must meet his Lord.

rise. like the sword of Khalid Bin Waleed
before it greeted the throat of the foe.

rise. like the fragrant tongue of Ali
as he recited poetry at his beloved's grave.

rise. like the gaze of the Muhammad (pbuh) as he
observed a majestic angel upon a humble horizon.

rise. like andalusia before it sold its keys.

rise. like the hip of a mother who carries
nations within her.

rise. rise. rise.

i know the power of my words

       yes, there is sincerity in my speech.

i grasp the strength in my silence

       there is eloquence in restraint.

why is it that a woman
who loves wholeheartedly
is often the one
most profoundly crushed?

why is it that the woman
who reveals the most skin
is most desired—yet most detested?

man must practice what he preaches
on the pulpits and preach
only that which he has practiced
one hundred times
before he sends a DM
      asks for a selfie
         a body
           a heart
              a soul.

man must understand
that women are daughters, sisters, and mothers
before anything else.

do you see these eyes?
some men may call them pretty.
i'd rather they call them insightful / deep / ruminating.
somewhere between a twinkle and a flash—
the windows to a faith that illuminates from within

Why is a woman who recognizes her worth considered "dangerous"? A *truly* dangerous woman is one who is broken and unhealed—not someone who walks with purpose and passion. In Islam, a woman who knows her value is empowered by her understanding of her worth in the eyes of Allah (swt), contributing positively to her surroundings rather than posing a threat.

What a tragedy it would be to discover your power at a point when it is too late to impart your service onto the world.

bondage disguised as freedom
is the belief that all that which is covered
must be oppressed and without choice.
and all that which is uncovered is free
and impervious to a predator's eyes.

Perhaps you have more power than you might think. Maybe if you only believed you could do it, you could *actually* do it. In essence, it is more about your willingness to accept your power than it is about the power itself. Take this as your sign to believe in yourself, to take that big step, and to put your trust in Allah (swt)—He will *never* fail you.

i come from the strength of a woman,
move to prayer
like the hips of a woman
came from struggle,
cried, then rose from the
embrace of a woman.
said "*zammilooni, zammilooni!*"
"cover me, cover me!"
in the arms of a woman.
received revelation
on the lap of a woman.
immaculate conception
in the womb of a woman.
prophets and messengers
raised by women.
migrated to madinah
and called on assertively
by the ansari women.

i move from self-doubt to strength,
from unworthy to worthy
from cute to absolutely phenomenal
from womb to womb.
this trait does not skip generations—
it's genetically coded
in each XX chromosome.
we do not rely on man—
we rely on God,
and man has no choice
but to follow.

i come from curved rib
—yes, under his arm,
but the rib protects *his* heart.
the rib stabilizes his spine,
he stands straight
because we fortified him,
taught him to read his ABC's

so he could learn how to vocalize his needs.
but weak is the spine that falls to desire.
when his woman is too strong for his limbs,
his heart resides in the *dunya*,
seeking her in every woman.
he will never find her.

I come from women
too strong to be contained in encyclopedias.
accolades so great
they do not fit into the prism
of societal expectation.
we have that untainted beauty
unexposed to industry
that tokenize / chew / then spit out politely
the *hijab*-wearing women.
let me tell you that the Muslim woman
is more than just her veil.
she is a tongue, two eyes,
and a conscious mind.
she wears a veil, yes.
and she wears
dignity,
integrity,
power,
and purpose.
this is how she moves.

blessed be the hand
that knows its power
does not come from the people—
it comes from the Creator
through the people.

Richness sits in the same hand that grasps onto faith like as if it is hot coal[47]. Poverty sits in the palms of the one who let go of the trustworthy handhold in order to amass the *dunya*.

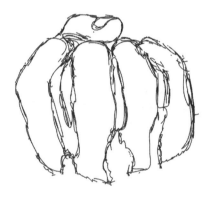

---

47. Anas ibn Malik reported: The Messenger of Allah (pbuh), said, "A time of patience will come to people in which adhering to one's religion is like grasping a hot coal." (Tirmidhi 2260)

The process of internal change initiates a transformation long before it manifests externally. This is because whatever you are internally convicted to will express itself in your outward actions. Islam teaches that sincere conviction and devotion in one's heart leads to righteous actions and behavior. As the Prophet Muhammad (pbuh) conveyed:

"Surely, there is a piece of flesh in the body, and when it becomes good (reformed), the whole body becomes good; but when it becomes corrupt, the whole body becomes corrupt. That piece of flesh is the heart." (Bukhari 52)

What does it feel like to be a Muslim woman, walking veiled through the summer heat? It's like traversing hot coals beneath the soles of my feet, navigating a blazing inferno where sweat beads roll down the sacred valleys of my forehead, forming a pearl ring along the curves of my skull—a halo-shaped crown ready to adorn me when no skin is on display.

It is akin to a clay oven, purifying sins, hoping this process leaves me sinless in a world where shamelessness is the new trend. Desire sits in a cage, waiting for a game, fed upon remembrance that fills souls and quenches lustful desires. It's about containing limits, remembering that disaster strikes when the ocean oversteps the earth, unleashing raging tsunamis and altering the course of lives.

I must remember that the way I dress carries weight beyond material wealth. This cloth has significance on the *mizaan* (the scales in the hereafter)—especially when tied to a sincere intention. Attraction, too, is a force of nature; it can become a wrecking ball when all men seek are trophy wives. Yet, if they are inclined to the outward appearance alone, it leaves a golden pool of those who appreciate you from within.

Guard the sanctity of your friendship group. If you observe the unbroken perfection of a circle, you will find it is whole, complete, and infinite. In the same way, let *your* circle be tight. The Prophet Muhammad (pbuh) emphasized the significance of good companionship, urging us to choose our friends wisely:

"*A man is upon the religion of his friend, so let one of you look at whom he befriends.*" (Tirmidhi 2378)

in the thickness of the night,
she peels away the frailty of her sleep
to stand before a Lord
who makes a grown man laugh then weep
she shushes her *nafs* back to slumber,
as her days are numbered.
and *dua* becomes incumbent upon her
like a fish that seeks the sea,
with a belly that holds a believer:

*la ilaha illa ant,subhaanaka inni
kuntu minath-dhalimeen*[48]

and she teaches it to her son,
so he knows that when he sins, there is hope,
even when he is enveloped in three layers of darkness.
"my son, know that God's mercy will prevail."
in disobedience to herself,
and obedience to her Maker,
she is worthy of the status of slave to her Creator.
she is master of her limbs—
especially what sits beneath the skull,
but above the jaw.
oh the joy that it brings to alleviate the bed springs
before dawn
has adorned the sky,
and the wolf has howled his last cry.
when the darkness is at its deepest,
and the brain is halted in a state between
sleepiness and awake—
that is where the dead soul can rise,
blossom, and achieve the highest of ranks,
because to thank God in these hours of most need
is like precious seeds watered by repentance
from a sinful deed.
and indeed, to be purged of all mistakes
is more worthy than a glorious

but futile existence.
i'd much rather live in a state
of constant resistance
than complacency and ease.

---

48. Prophet Yunus (as), known in English as "Jonah", is a revered figure in Islamic tradition. The supplication (*dua*) he made is documented in the Quran: "La ilaha illa ant, subhaanaka inni kuntu minath-dhalimeen," which translates to "There is no deity except You; exalted are You. Indeed, I have been of the wrongdoers." (The Quran, 21:87)

Prophet Yunus (as) found himself in a challenging situation when he decided to leave his people without waiting for Allah's (swt) permission to do so. As a consequence, he was swallowed by a whale. In the depths of darkness within the belly of the sea creature, Yunus (as) realized the gravity of his mistake and turned to Allah (swt) in sincere repentance.

In this critical moment, Yunus (as) humbly uttered the powerful *dua*, acknowledging the oneness and greatness of Allah (swt), seeking His forgiveness, and admitting his own wrongdoing. This heartfelt supplication reflects the essence of repentance and reliance on the mercy of the Most Merciful.

Allah (swt), in His infinite compassion, accepted Prophet Yunus' (as) repentance, and the whale eventually released him. This story serves as a profound lesson in humility, repentance, and the boundless mercy of Allah (swt). It underscores the idea that turning to Allah (swt) with a sincere heart, even in the darkest moments, can lead to forgiveness and redemption.

Relying on people invites disappointment. Depending on Allah (swt) fortifies the spirit, coloring you in a confidence that may appear strange to others. They are amazed by it, even if they do not fully understand it.

One of the greatest triumphs of *Shaytaan* is to create dissension and division among family members. This is why the strength of a society hinges on the strength of the families that comprise it. Allah (swt) says:

"Do they not see that Allah extends provision for whom He wills and restricts [it]? Indeed, in that are signs for a people who believe. So give the relative his right, as well as the needy and the traveler. That is best for those who desire the countenance of Allah, and it is they who will be the successful." (The Quran, 30:37-38)

be *soft*, be strong

know your worth—
then act accordingly

.

ABOUT THE AUTHOR

Kashmir Maryam is an author and poet who is turning heads in the literary world with her unique insights on mindfulness, spirituality, and personal growth. Born in England and of Kashmiri heritage, her books "The Muslim Woman's Manifesto," "Nafsi," and "The Muslim Woman's Journal" offer a fresh perspective on the intersection of spirituality and modern life. Through her guidance on self-care, inner peace, and finding purpose and meaning, she has helped countless readers discover the transformative power of personal growth and spiritual fulfillment.

www.kashmirmaryam.com
www.instagram.com/kashmirmaryam
www.tiktok.com/kashmirmaryam

MORE FROM KASHMIR

The Muslim Woman's Manifesto
*10 Steps to Achieving Phenomenal
Success, in Both Worlds*

❧❧

The Muslim Woman's Journal
*A Book of Reflective Writing Prompts to Inspire a
Successful Mindset, a Life Brimming with Purpose
& a Deeper Connection to Allah*

❧❧

Nafsi
Jihad upon my Self
(poetry)

Made in United States
Troutdale, OR
09/26/2024

23155227R00159